i write

Frank Oxarart

I WRITE. Copyright © 2025 by the estate of Frank Oxarart. Edited by Christina Oxarart. All rights reserved. Printed in the United States of America. No part of this book may be used or reproduced in any manner whatsoever without written permission except in the case of brief quotations embodied in critical articles and reviews. For information address Outrun Press, 212 Long Hill Road, Hillsborough, NJ 08844.

ISBN: 978-0-9965996-3-4

Library of Congress Control Number: 2025941114

contents

I Write	1
My First Appointment	3
Family Photo #1	5
With Apologies to Honoré de Balzac	7
Attitude Versus DNA	9
The Vineyard	11
Shy Walls	13
Daily Prayers	15
My First Car	17
Donald J.	19
Fate	21
Annual Physical	23
The Time Traveler	25
For Sylvie	27
Sitting in the Library	29
First Kiss	31
Rehearsal Dinner	33
Still	35
Seasons? What Seasons?	37
When Did We Get So Tired of Death	39
It Wasn't for the Sex	41
Google This	45
Stolen Hours	47
Islands	49
Venus de Milo	51
A Judgmental Life	53
Ode to Paper	55
Blue	57
Evening Prayer	59
Angel	61
Fourth of July, 2020	63
The Daily Dinner Dishes	65

God Made Man	67
A Love Story	69
Woe is Poe	73
Breakfast	75
How Are You Doing?	77
Intelligent Design	79
Embarrassed	81
Pinocchio	83
Sisyphus Retires	85
My Body	87
The Peoples of the World	89
Pop	91
A.I. as Poet	93
In Appreciation	95
A Villanelle for Tom	97
We The People	99
Kalaulau Valley	101
Happy Birthday	103
Guilty	105
Poetry	107
No Need	109
My Brother Bob	111
Tracking My Day	113
Let Me Tell You	115
Melody de Amor	117
A TV Blessing	119
What Time Is It?	121
"Pop's gone"	123
Tried and True	125
Hometown	127
Progress	129
Staying in Touch	131
Wisdom of the Aged	133
Meditation at Marin	135
What If	137
A Bland Life	141
Apologies to Walt	143

i write

I WRITE to know me
   not the persona
   presented to others
   not the image created
   for others the facade
   so carefully crafted
   even I don't know
   the true me.

I write quickly
   rapidly
   mindlessly
   not stopping
   outrunning
   the guardian editor within
   until truth spills from the pen
   as if written in blood.

I write
   feelings and thoughts

unheard before
surprising the writer
whose tears
dilute the lifeink
flowing onto the page.
I write to know me.

my first appointment

SO small
    I can not
    even breathe
    curled up
    in total darkness
    my heart beats
    in rhythm
    within the walls
    that confine me

a restrictive shelter
    without windows
    a tiny entrance
    too small to exit

wave-like contractions
    increase in intensity
    insistently push me
    unbearable pressure

Frank Oxarart

until a sharp blade
    the wall of my too-tight room
    frees me from my sanctuary
    lifts me into the light of life
    frees me from my mother's womb

family photo #1

AN INDISTINCT FIGURE
    Barely two inches tall
    Resplendent in a long frock coat
    Brimmed hat held low in his hand.

This figure fading from memory
    In two countries
    Sojourned in Argentina
    On his way to the Golden State
    From his native France.

He found his fortune
    Not in the ground of the 49ers
    But of the ground
    Raising crops and livestock
    Planted his seed, watched it grow.

One grew into a sepia-toned son
    Standing on locomotive steps

Still just three inches tall
Ready to extend the journey.

A journey given fresh impetus
　By the first life-size member
　We have known
　The tiny figures who came before
　Take on personality and purpose
　Through this full-grown embodiment

Which gives meaning and context
　To our family
　As we continue along the path
　Destined to become faded shrinking pictures
　For future generations.

with apologies to honoré de balzac

PREPARING FOR THE BATTLE AHEAD, the first stop is at Starbucks or Peets. Not content with Balzac's simple espresso-like stimulant, the order is for an individualized, customized blend, choice of milk, added flavors, multi-sized seasonal variances. Yet just as with Balzac, though not at the rate of fifty cups per day, caffeine flows into our stomachs, fires up all of our mental processes. Long buried memories stir up previously unthought-of brilliant concepts. Ink flows, slowly at first, then in an outpouring as plot lines develop, characters emerge, filling out the new notions. *Were it not for coffee one could not write, which is to say one could not live.*

attitude versus dna

A FAMILIAR STRANGER looks at me
    from the mirror each day
    features not uniquely mine
    the thin blue eyes stare
    at familial earlobes
    melding into the puffiness
    along my jawbone
    more and more I recognize
    my father looking back at me.

I reach to touch his face once more
    the hand reaching is his as well.

All I see in me comes from my father
    his body, a little taller, thinner
    even my mind seems to work like his
    that Basque twist of looking at things
    striving for his eternal optimism.

Frank Oxarart

Body, mind and soul come from my father
    what do I carry from my mother?

Attitude.

A way of looking at myself and others
    distancing myself from them
    observing rather than participating
    judging instead of accepting
    looking down on their frivolity as childish.

Standing off to the side
    lonely in the midst of many
    I judge myself and others
    find I am lacking as well.

Who looks back from the mirror each morning?
    The created me or the creative me?

the vineyard

GNARLED vines spread outward
    ancient roots buried on a hillside
    clusters of grapes burst forth
    from nodes along the branches.

Grapes grow plump and rich
    in the warmth of the sun
    nourished by lifegiving moisture
    pulled from the harsh ground.

Many grapes, often of different varieties
    go into vats where they ferment, evolve over time
    into the invigorating, intoxicating nectar of life
    others, less fortunate, are left behind.

Frank Oxarart

Isolated under the sun's heat
    all lifegiving moisture driven out
    leaving a dry, wrinkled reminder
    of what once could have been.

shy walls

SHYNESS IS like a wall
 too high and wide
 to get around.
 A wall in my mind
 erected by others
 brick by brick
 when I was too small
 to say no.
 As I grew larger
 the wall did too.
 I did nothing
 to dismantle it.
 Now as big as I am,
 too big for my mind,
 encompassing my
 entire being.
 Shutting me down,
 closing me out,
 isolating me,
 leaving only,
 me.

daily prayers

PRAY for a healthy baby
    Pray for good grades
    Pray for a raise in pay
    Pray for a better job
    Pray she will love me
    Pray for nourishing rain
    Pray for the rain to stop
    Pray for good physical exams
    Pray the cancer will go away
    Pray for good news
    Pray for a home run
    Pray our team will win
    Pray for our soldiers in harm's way
    Pray for victory
    Pray for survival

The air is filled with prayers
    In all languages
    Listen closely to the cacophony
    Of foreign voices praying
    For their way of life

Frank Oxarart

    Praying in all religions
    Praying they will prevail

Whose prayers does God hear
    Whose prayers does He fulfill
    Whose side is He on

my first car

A '34 CHEVY COUPE two years younger than I was
    freedom to roam freeway free Southern California

Balboa for Spring Break   side trips to Knott's Berry Farm
    Dizzy's bent trumpet bebop jazz at Pasadena Civic
    Hermosa Beach/abalone steaks/jazz at the Lighthouse
    Olvera Street/taquitos   Santa Monica Pier/just because
    western swing at the Palamino in the Valley
    anything musical at the Hollywood Bowl
    body surfing the turbulent Wedge at Newport
    parking on Mulholland Drive above 77 Sunset Strip
    (which doesn't exist)

nothing was ever too far   knew how to get everywhere
    the roads etched into my heart.

Even today I can give you clear directions just as I learned them
    stay on this street until you pass where
    the little red school house used to be

Frank Oxarart

the road splits at the old Sears Roebuck
don't go right   glitzy strip malls and car dealers
go left up through the poppy fields
and old groves of olive trees
past the abandoned priest factory
(the brothers grew vegetables there)
when you get to Bob's Big Boy Drive-in
(closed now)
your destination is on the left

These days my latest ride is sleek and modern
    its disembodied voice   male or female   my choice
    cuts into the sports scores to advise me
    slow traffic in the right lane two miles ahead
    horns in on a soaring Chet Baker cool west coast jazz solo
    stay in the left lane   merging traffic on the right
    intrudes on saloon singer Sinatra as he flies me to the moon
    you have arrived at your destination

I miss that little red school house
    and where it used to be.

donald j.

TODAY HAS BECOME like every other
    Rife with deception and fear mongering
    Unaccustomed to such demeanor
    Machiavellian in its deceitful nature
    Patriotism given way to latent Tribalism
    Instilling seemingly irreconcilable hostility
    So that I no longer comprehend
    My country: *one nation indivisible*
                      with liberty and justice for all.

fate

I.

She had lost her way running
    in a park in Eugene, Oregon,
    ran into a man she had worked with
    a few years earlier and
    he drove her back to town.

Flying back to Los Angeles,
    she wondered why fate
    would put her in that situation.
    He had been her least favorite person.
    Decided that she was meant
    to get back in touch with those
    she had liked from that time.

II.

I've got a funny story to tell you she said.
    I said to tell me at lunch, if she was free.
    We both told our stories
    bringing each other up to date
    on what had happened in our lives
    since we had worked together.

Later that day, I called her,
    told her how much I had enjoyed it.
    She said she had too.
    Let's do it again sometime I said.
    She said she would like that.
    How about tomorrow I said.
    She said she had an appointment.
    Break it I said.
    She said okay.

Later, we both said
    I do.

annual physical

BLOOD PRESSURE
   normal

pulse
   normal

breathe in   breathe out
   a flat tentacled disc
    moves across my chest
        normal

thump my cavities
    press my abdomen
    probe for hernia
       normal

blood tests   all good

LCL a little high
otherwise

all is normal
    for a man my age

is that good?

the time traveler

TRAVELING centuries into the past
    I stood the center of attention
    as people marveled
    though somewhat skeptically
    at my tales of the future

at how man flew like birds
    sailed beneath the seas like fish
    how pictures flew through the air
    how man flew through space
    exploring other worlds in our sky

how everyone had their own
    handheld knowledge device
    enabling instant communication
    spreading knowledge and understanding
    of other people's cultures and beliefs
    accepted our differences

how that understanding and acceptance
    spread universal love and peace
    within our common humanity

how I lied
    oh how I lied

for sylvie

October 28, 1948 - August 7, 2009

THE SUN ROSE this morning
    as it does every morning
    light splashing over earth's darkness
    life's constant rhythm of rebirth

Sylvie passed away today
    left her husband inconsolable
    friends and family mourned as well

We needed a split-second pause
    a slight worldwide stutter
    time to say *au revoir*

just for Sylvie

sitting in the library

ESCAPE
    Sail the seas
    In a two masted schooner
    Flee from pirates
    Be the pirate
    Dive beneath ice floes
    Trek jungle paths
    Find a way
    Through the desert
    Lift yourself
    Foot by foot
    To the highest peak
    Soar on thermal currents
    Blast through the atmosphere
    Become the man on the moon
    Stalk the dark streets
    Searching for the guilty
    Save fair maiden
    The city, the world
    Sign the document
    That saves the world

Turn the pages.

first kiss

I DON'T REMEMBER my first kiss.
    There have been many,
    given and received.

My mother and father
    kissed me first,
    Probably.

There were aunts and cousins,
    with welcoming kisses,
    that was their way.

Later, I gave kisses, pecks really.
    "Kiss grandma hello."
    "Kiss your cousin goodbye."

My father was in his seventies,
    when I first kissed him for real,

often since then.

I don't know when
    I will give the first
    heartfelt kiss
   to my mother.

rehearsal dinner

OKAY, places everyone.
    This is a rehearsal for Sunday.
    Peter, slide in a little tighter.
    Andrew, sit next to your brother.
    John, James, on the other side.
    Six on the left, six on the right.

Mary, you can stay right there,
    we can edit you out later.

Someone keep the wine goblets filled.
    Don't worry, we won't run out,
    not as long as there's water around.
    Didn't anyone get a haircut?
    And what's with all the brown robes?
    Try to be more colorful on Sunday.

Judas, quit counting your coins,
    J.C. is picking up the tab for all of us.

still

Still
yet to be
born from the womb
delivered into a caring world
nurtured by loving mother and father
raised protectively within a global society
connected to similar unknown souls worldwide
achieved others' dreams set down long before birth
fulfilled the promise of success made to family and friends
fulfilled the destiny preordained by powers beyond his own
achieved meaningless tasks that benefited no one
connected only with those within his close circle
raised offspring of his own making and
nurtured them as he had been
delivered longtime goals
born thru the years
yet now is
still

seasons? what seasons?

GROWING up in ever warm L.A.
    under the Southern California sun,
        Winter, Spring, Summer or Fall - what's Autumn?
    I have always been vague about "seasons".

My seasons were more meaningful,
    football season, basketball season,
    year-round surfing season.
    Summer time was beach time.
    Skin burned olive by the sun's fire.

One January, at Ft. Devens, Mass,
    as a young, olive-clad draftee,
    assigned as overnight "fire watch",
    I dutifully patrolled our barracks area
    during the bone-chilling snowy night,
    alert to any potential fire danger,
    protecting my buddies as they slept.

Frank Oxarart

Rousted from bed by morning reveille
    my comrades-in-arm were forced
    to endure ice-cold showers,
    the banked coal fires in the boilers
    having died out during the night.
    Coal? What's a boiler anyway?

It wasn't my fault! What did they expect?
    Assigning a warm weather, beach going,
    body surfing Southern Californian
    to a duty nothing in life
    had prepared him for?

What else was I not prepared for?

when did we get so tired of death

I ONLY HAVE to think back to 9/11
    as two airlines impaled the Twin Towers
    steel and glass structures collapsed
    an instant grave for 3000 Americans

We rose up in righteous anger
    unleashed shock and awe and death
    2500 American soldiers lost their lives
    thousands more mutilated in body and mind
    as our longest war ever continues

Add George Floyd to death's roll call
    one in a stream of racial serial killings
    a knee ended his breath of life
    sparked days weeks months of outrage
    protests in cities and towns across the country
    thousands young and old all colors
    braved the crowds demanded justice

Frank Oxarart

Today under attack by an unseen enemy
    people take refuge in their homes
    watch as TV talking heads keep count
    500,000 Americans and counting
    have breathed their last

No war has been declared
    no all-out mobilization of resistance
    where is our moral outrage
    our national sense of unquenchable grief
    people protesting enough is enough

When did we get so tired of death

it wasn't for the sex

IT WASN'T for the sex that I knew you
    Sex wasn't the driving force
    It was a way to become intimate
    A way to feel close as our bodies entwined
    Our minds and souls mingled in the aftermath.

I found me in you, not because I was in you
    But because in your opening to me physically
    I was able to open myself to you
    My thoughts, desires, dreams and aspirations.

I was more me in you than without you
    I never knew who and what I could be
    Before immersing myself in you.

In our measured rhythms
    Giving to each other
    We discovered ourselves
    Found the completeness

Frank Oxarart

We had each been missing.

As we lie together I am taller
    Than I have ever been
    Held by your legs and arms
    I am freer than ever before
    Our dialogue more complete
    Than words could ever make it.

My body is larger having joined
    With your body
    My heart fuller having opened
    To yours.

Our coupling, meant for birthing a child,
    Gave birth to a full-grown, emerging, evolving, adult
    One who loves you fully and freely
    In opening myself to you,
    I opened myself to me as well
    Know me as well as you know me.

No, it isn't for the sex that I know you
    It's through our sexual union I found myself.

It Wasn't for the Sex

No, it was not and is not for the sex,
   But Lord,
   The sex is good.

google this

WE LIVE in an age of instant communication
    Cell phones, smartphones, the internet
    Computers, laptops, notebooks
    Facebook, Twitter, LinkedIn

Yet we are more fractionalized
    More contact yet more isolated
    More what happened, less why
    Or how it affects us

Our air crisscrossed by electrical fields
    Bluetooth, WiFi, airplane mode
    Carrying messages to our bodies
    What does it carry to our bodies

All the knowledge of the universe
    In perpetual flight around the world
    Available to anyone from anyone
    No vetting as to its veracity

Frank Oxarart

Facebook, Twitter, Skype, GPS
    Mass communication for the masses
    Are we more connected to our world or
    More isolated in our easy availability

In spite of this virulent, viral communication
    Have we so splintered ourselves
    We no longer can build a community
    Much less a ship of state

stolen hours

STOLEN HOURS, stolen days,
    more time to dig within,
    down to those thoughts
    I seldom speak.

Time stolen from others,
    my work, my family,
    other responsibilities,
    just time alone with me.

It was not always so.
    There were times, before,
    when I would not
    spend time with myself.

Hiding from the light
    of self-examination,
    afraid to be alone,
    Not wanting to see.

Frank Oxarart

Spending time alone
    comes easier now,
    with no other purpose
    but to be.

My day passes,
    no hour hand on the clock,
    only the darkening sky,
    shows this time alone,
    is drawing to a close.

I enjoy these moments,
    alone in my own company,
    learning to listen to myself,
    listening to hidden thoughts
    only we can hear.

islands

WE ALL LIVE on mountain tops
    Islands

rising through the blue waters
    that cover connecting valleys

    Islands

separated by oceans
    of misunderstanding.

venus de milo

GODDESS of love and beauty
    lives alone in the Louvre
    born of the gods
    she rebelled against Zeus
    chose Ares God of War
    then Eros God of Love
    later the mortal Adonis

poised demurely draped
    head held high her eyes search
    in vain for her next conquest

her body forever sensual
    shoulders soft and smooth
    smallish impudent breasts
    an arousing curve of the hips
    I once cupped in the hollow of my hands

those missing arms encircled me

    her hands lovingly clutched my back
    holding me as tightly as I held her

I assume it was the gods' jealousy
    that drove them to separate us
    tearing me from her so violently

I sit alone now
    Gerry Mulligan's cool jazz rhythmic
    Venus de Milo plays in the background
    comforted knowing
    her arms will never hold another
    as they once held me

a judgmental life

OUR MOTHER HAD SEEN sixty-five as a finish line
    time to put life down and coast
    spent her next thirty-five years
    sitting at home in quiet judgment

She had been a lifelong observer
    found others inadequate in some way
    taught her three sons to stand back
    not get involved   not participate

It was almost a relief
    when she entered her parallel life
    one embedded in the past
    seldom the present
    fearing the future

She asked for her youngest son
    wouldn't accept the grown man
    who cared for her every day

Frank Oxarart

    demanded the younger version
    from the picture on the mantle
    not the impertinent one
    who insisted she take her pills
    who cooked her meals
    who bathed and dressed her
    who gave her thirty years from his life
    she gave him life   took half of it back

Her other two sons made occasional duty calls
    invented reasons to leave   as they walked in
    lived their own lives   raised their own families
    freed from her negative judgmental attitude

Concerned what the neighbors would think
    neighbors she deigned to know
    she passed away in silent sleep
    afraid to go any other way

ode to paper

VIRGINAL,
    blank, stark white,
    waiting to be impregnated,
    anxious to spring
    to life.
    Generations can be
    outlined,
    filled out,
    on the never-ending role.
    Note thoughts
    passed from one
    to another.
    Document deeds
    not to be forgotten.
    Pass on stirrings and spice
    to enrich
    the family fare.
    Attest to new members,
    not born,
    acquired,
    assimilated.
    The whole becoming

stronger
from the union.

Pages large as the sky
    pulsate with life.
    Shouts of victory
    and pain,
    tears of joy and defeat,
    sadness and loss.
    Often intermingled,
    passed generation to
    Generation.
    Strengthening the family
    fabric,
    Woven strand by strand
    as the paper is.
    A never ending canvas
    chronicling our lives.

blue

BLUE, blue, blue
    Hooray for the
    Red, white and blue

Boys of the Union
    Wore blue
    Spilled the red
    Of their brothers
    In gray
    Left them sad
    Depressed
    Hid their melancholy
    Behind bawdy behavior

These blue collar men
    Wore working man's blue jeans
    Ate the blue plate special
    Never owned a blue chip stock
    Dreamed of sailing the blue sea
    Chasing the blue whale

Frank Oxarart

Longed for the bluegrass of home
With its bluebells, bluebirds and
Blueberries

Lay still beneath the trees
    Staring up at the blue sky
    Red spreading from
    Their cold, white skins
    Turning blue.

evening prayer

OUR FATHER
    who art in Heaven
    we thank Thee
    for creating us
    in your image

We praise Thee
    for creating this
    perfect world
    we choose to control

A world where
    disease runs rampant
    where hunger afflicts many
    where greed gluttony pride
    are rewarded

A world where men
    created in Your image

kill one another
in Your name

A world where the race
    is not to the deserving or needy
    but to the privileged
    who stand on the necks
    of their brethren

A world we cannot live in
    follow just ten simple rules
    replace them with volumes
    of laws we choose for ourselves

You chose to create
    this perfect world
    with imperfect people
    who live for themselves
    not in harmony with others

Our Father
    Hollow be Thy name

angel

I ONCE MET an angel
    in Tombstone, Arizona
    near Ft. Huachuca

Angel Baldenegro
    a latter-day successor to Wyatt Earp
    infamous for the gunfight at the OK Corral

built like a wrestler
    tall thick body long arms
    ebony skin dressed in black
    virtually invisible at night

amiable by nature patient
    though papa to six little angels

Angel kept the peace in Tombstone
    broken one night

Frank Oxarart

outside the Crystal Palace Saloon
an off-duty soldier tequila drunk
fired his six-shooter into the night sky

Angel politely asked for his gun
    instead the soldier fired at Angel
    he never flinched as the bullet hit
    walked forward   reaching for the pistol

The soldier dropped his weapon
    ran as fast as he could
    to the jail
    demanding he be locked up
    safe from the avenging Angel

Tombstone was once again peaceful
    stayed that way as Angel walked the streets

Later I traded khakis for civvies
    gave my burro Pedro to Angel
    for his six kids to ride
    my gift to the first angel I ever met.

fourth of july, 2020

1776 THE YEAR we started
    declared ourselves a free people
    declared *all men are created equal*
    free from the tyranny of the British King

1776 the year we pursued a promise
    by an earlier English King   The Magna Carta
    protected the rights of the church
    protected the rights of the barons
    provided justice for some
    yet not for all

1776 the year thirteen states united
    fought to further those freedoms
    over the next 200 plus years
    extend the benefits of freedom
    to all our citizens
    on paper

2016   the year we went back
    not the yellow gold of the English Crown
    but the shallow yellow crown of Trump
    who promised to *Make America Great Again*
    who would take us to an even earlier 1776

1776 BC   the Code of Hammurabi
    his laws over all   though not all the same
    three classes
    superiors   commoners   slaves

2016   the year of a Trumpian Code
    laws for himself
    declared by himself
    our Constitution   ignored
    our Declaration of Independence
    ignored

2020   the year we can hit
    Restart

the daily dinner dishes

STANDING HERE in our kitchen
    arm-deep in soapy water
    washing tonight's dinner dishes

I think of all the dishes
    that I have washed
    our dinner detritus

the many other kitchens
    Santa Monica to San Francisco
    stops in New York Westport Sarasota
    your first kitchen in West L.A.

I slipped past your threshold
    hung my suit shirt and tie
    behind your bedroom door

you cleared a drawer for me

Frank Oxarart

room on your bathroom counter
for my toothbrush and razor

we sat holding hands
    on your blue couch
I held my breath

elated when you said yes
    committing me to a lifetime
    doing our daily dinner dishes

god made man

GOD MADE Man in His own image,
    why do we see Man in our image,
    as if we were God?

In truth we are each little Gods,
    every Man created in our own image
    thus a part of each of us.

Why then do we focus
    on insignificant differences
    to set us apart?

a love story

NOBLE CAESAR STANDS PROUDLY
    on the dewy Connecticut lawn
    wearing his sleek black coat
    head up back straight
    all four feet firmly on the ground

This morning as every morning
    white apricot-tinged Candy
    races from her home to join him
    on their daily patrol around the grounds
    surrounding their masters' homes
    her sparkling eyes embrace him
    his sideway glance betrays
    his affection for her

Tragically Caesar will be moving away
    leaving Candy behind however
    a surrogate for Caesar
    proposes to Candy's parents

Frank Oxarart

an arranged marriage

So on a bright sunny day
    two little girls give Candy
    a garland of flowers around her head
    to Caesar clad in a white polo shirt
    and now   joined in matrimony
    Candy will join Caesar in their new home

They travel to Colorado
    hike the Sangre de Cristo mountains
    chase deer   avoid bears   and mountain lions
    an unfortunate encounter with a porcupine
    then on to Marin County
    chase more deer and wild turkeys
    every day their life together a joyful adventure
    every night they sleep nuzzling each other
    they are inseparable   until one day

A malignancy growing in Candy
    finally consumes her
    Separates her from her Caesar

The tumor that has devoured Candy's body
    tears Caesar's heart apart as well

Through his grief he continues his daily patrols
    though clearly his enthusiasm has faded
    his wounded heart weakens   until
    on a fog-shrouded day in Marin
    Caesar goes in search of Candy

A Love Story

And if you look into the Marin sky at night
    a little behind the constellation of Orion
    you may see Canis Caesar and Canis Candy
    on patrol   together again   forever

woe is poe

I **ONCE SAT** high upon a bust of Athena
    angels danced around me in the air
    in the midnight cold of dreary December
    my shadow flickered lightly on the floor
    floating over that of one whose suffering
    was deep and unquenchable

He questioned from whence I came
    a messenger from God in heaven
    or the keeper of the underworld
    I would not answer could not answer
    offered instead an ancient potion
    meant to ease grief and suffering
    he misunderstood my tender kiss
    felt instead I had pierced his heart

As I sat on Athena's bust above the chamber door
    looking down past his desolation and loneliness
    I saw reflected in the mirror above the hearth

the source of his pain that rare and radiant maiden
that sainted maiden Lenore
it was then I finally spoke

Evermore

breakfast

THE WINDOWS ARE STEAMED fog-like
    Blurring the familiar scene inside
    I know what I will find
    When I push through the door

Round stools lining the ancient counter
    Red faux leather bench seats
    Bracket-scarred tables
    The air heavy with familiar odors

My mind wakes as the first sip
    Of coffee, no sugar, a little cream
    Brightens my taste buds in anticipation
    Of eggs over easy, crisp bacon
    Sourdough toast buttered lightly
    Ready for sweet strawberry jam
    Then more caffeine, a large orange juice
    My morning ritual indulgence

Frank Oxarart

A familiar opening
    To another bright new day
    Full of promise
    Waiting to be seized
    All things seem possible
    As I fuel the furnace
    That will carry me through
    The travails that lie ahead

This day builds on all those before
    Successful or not, mortared into place
    By this most important event in my day
    One I will happily replicate many times
    As my lifeline grows longer
    Bringing memories of all those earlier

Breakfast
    Another new beginning

how are you doing?

A SIMPLE GREETING
    asked most every day,
    not expecting an answer
    might not listen if given.

Maybe the answer gives hope
    things can get better
    or a secret guilty feeling
    since you are better off.

How am I doing?
    Do you really want to know?
    Do you actually care?

Pieces of me keep dying.
    My father, my mother,
    older, to be expected, but
    my younger brother,
    an expiration date

that came too soon.

How am I doing?

Just fine thanks.
    Thanks for asking.

How are you doing?

intelligent design

MINUTES BECOME hours
    Hours become days, then years
    Years become as hours

Our hearts tick to the metronome
    Of a clock's constant countdown
    Never knowing the final tick

In between
    Life
    As we know it

Seeking some grander purpose
    To our existence in the universe
    Wanting to make a difference
    No proof that anything matters

Still faith in some ultimate design

Planned by an omniscient being
Who guides us with divine light
Yet allows fragmentation, separation
Destruction of those who disagree
With their way, as the only way

How in God's name
   Could any intelligent being
   Design a world like that?

embarrassed

I HAVE to confess
    I just wanted a peek
    catch you unaware
    in the steamy bathroom
    standing in the shower
    breasts rising and falling
    as your arms rose and fell
    washing your shoulder-length hair

I don't deny it
    When you turned
    caught me
    I blushed
    all over
    slightly embarrassed
    totally aroused

Frank Oxarart

my eyes focused
    on your bare shoulders
    smooth and seductive
    as when I first saw you

spinning down the hallway
    tanned tantalizing shoulders
    in your red peasant blouse
    matching full skirt swirling

the wedding dress bared
    your enticing shoulders
    just as that pink negligee
    displayed their promise

I have to confess
    I have a lifelong thirst for you
    that does not embarrass me

pinocchio

GEPPETTO THE WOODCARVER made Pinocchio
    Then freed him from his strings
    Made him human
    With all the human faults
    With a built-in fault detector
    A nose that grows and grows
    As lie upon lie is told

If Geppetto had fashioned Congress
    And assorted politicians of our day
    As he did Pinocchio
    If he had carved the business leaders
    Of our time then freed them
    They would walk around in the shadow
    Of their own noses
    Possibly with wheels to support
    The farthest extremity
    Noses they could joust with
    As they sought their own way

Geppetto freed the puppets
    By making them like a real boy
    Humanizing them to follow
    Their own proclivities
    Though not always civilly
    Freed them to make puppets
    Of the rest of us

Where is Jiminy Cricket when we need him?

sisyphus retires

THROUGHOUT THE AGES, ageless Sisyphus
    arose each morning
    bent his shoulder to his task
    focused on the goal at hand
    pushed his burden steadily uphill
    to the summit of the mountain
    only to have it roll back down
    at the end of each day

Still every morning he got up
    took up his chore anew
    eyes staring straight ahead
    unfazed by his task's enormity
    never questioning its purpose
    never resting until completion
    of his daily eternal struggle

Until one day, he stopped
    took in the world around him
    a world he had largely ignored

unchanged by his ongoing travail
then setting aside his daily duty
he breathed a sigh of relief

Today Sisyphus sits with Atlas
    who earlier had shrugged *his* duties
    relaxing in their neighborhood Starbucks
    sipping on their flavored decaf lattes
    watching others continue
    their Sisyphus-like life.

my body

I WAS BORN into a body
    I will never own
    It has been my task
    to care for this home
    I lease for my soul
    a task not always
    taken seriously.

A strong fragile vessel
    subject to many ailments
    brought on by the smallest
    of unseen invaders
    preventive maintenance
    was my assigned duty
    one I often shirked.

As years went by I grew
    not only in body
    but in knowledge as well
    some lessons learned hard

others I hardly was
aware I was learning
everything around me
had an effect on me
too often ignored.

Knowing what I know now
    I should have taken better care
    of my earthly body
    knowing what we know now
    shouldn't we take better care
    of this body of earth.

the peoples of the world

MANY YEARS AGO, the peoples of the world
    United with a common language
    Set forth to build a tower
    A tower that would reach the heavens

As the tower rose it created
    Great consternation among the gods
    "if as one people speaking the same language
    they have begun to do this then nothing they plan to do
    will be impossible for them"

So in their infinite wisdom the gods
    Imposed many different languages on the people
    And they scattered around the world
    Dissolving their previous, precious unity
    Their common purpose

Now this Tower of Babel has come to us
    To our nation's capitol, splintering our unity

Frank Oxarart

Who has given us this blue and red language
Who has created the differences in understanding
So that we seem to have lost our common purpose
Through an increasing inability to communicate
What then becomes of our once united peoples.

pop

LIVING in a strange land
    Hours and miles away
    True to his own language
    He lived an earlier life
    In countless stories told
    People he had known
    Careers he had built
    Family that he created
    He stayed young through
    His boys and their deeds
    Ever positive no matter what
    Bright future lying just ahead
    No setback anything but momentary
    He regretted nothing unless
    He could change it
    Otherwise move on
    Make the best of it
    He accepted his fate
    As if chosen
    Lived his life with
    Strength and vigor and joy
    Until his body failed him

Frank Oxarart

Never his mind or heart
Lives on in his sons
Some of who know him
And grandchildren who
Should have known him better
A choice he made
A choice imposed by circumstance
His life was full
But not full enough

a.i. as poet

> AI could one day develop a soul: the word we use
> for each person's idea of what they are and why.
> *Marvin Minsky, MIT*

MIDWAY upon the journey of our life
    I met a traveler from an antique land
    Bent double, like old beggars under sacks,
    Because I could not stop for Death –
    I will arise and go now, and go to Innisfree.
    The curfew tolls the knell of parting day.

The Moving Finger writes; and having writ
    She walks in beauty, like the night
    How do I love thee? Let me count the ways.
    Shall I compare thee to a summer's day?
    Drink to me only with thine eyes,
    Gather ye rosebuds while ye may.

When I consider how my light is spent

Frank Oxarart

Since you ask, most days I cannot remember.
The world is too much with us: late and soon,
Had we but world enough, and time.
O friends, no more these sounds!
Breathes there a man with soul so dead,
Do not go gentle into that good night.

Source: *The 100 Best Poems of All Time* edited by Leslie Pockell.

in appreciation

STANDING THERE IN THE LIGHT,
    he could feel it.
    The end of his world approaching,
    as steadily as the hands of a clock
    counting down the minutes
    until all he knew would cease to be.

A rhythmic sound rose from the
    darkness formed by the light,
    growing louder and stronger
    pulsing in time with his heart.
    Eyes misting, he strained to see
    beyond the void before him.

As the minutes passed
    he tried to remember
    what he was,
    who he was,
    how he had come
    to this moment.

Frank Oxarart

The hour had passed.
    His had too, he realized,
    Looking down at the face
    of the shiny new watch,
    hands circling monotonously,
    mirroring the downward spiral of his life.

a villanelle for tom

A VILLANELLE no less with pleasure the subject
    Villanelles have all these rules about repetition
    I never liked repetition   don't mind revisiting
    There are several actual villas I would like to revisit

Such as the first one in Entrechaux in Provence
    Near Vaisonne-la-Romaine with its vestiges of Rome
    Though truthfully it was actually a farmhouse
    Or in Merida in the Yucatan Peninsula
    With its indoor patio pool   Uber rides everywhere

Then how about the Villa above Nice
    Where I expected Hercule Poirot any moment
    And Madame Olivier spoiled us with over a dozen
    Homemade jams from the surrounding trees

My favorite might be Villa Vignamaggio
    In Greve in the Chianti region of Italy
    Near the David and other wonders of Florence

Kenneth Branagh Emma Thompson and Denzel
Had just finished filming "Much Ado About Nothing"
At the Villa   now that was something

But my true favorite is the Villa above St. Tropez
    With family and friends invited for my birthday
    24 croissants from the bakery each morning
    A dozen plain and a dozen au chocolat
    Hoped to see Brigitte Bardot strolling the streets
    As we played Petanque in the square
    Or sat sipping Pastis eyeing the yachts in the harbor

It has all been about pleasure
    Though not in a Villanelle
    Sorry Tom.

we the people

PEOPLE SIT, rapt
    In their thoughts
    Their hopes and dreams
    Pulsing through their bodies
    Waiting for some great truth
    To burst forth
    Solve all their concerns

People wait, patiently
    For some small hint
    As to who will lead them
    Through the fire and uncertainty
    Of their questioning lives
    Who will bring stability
    And sanity to their world

People watch and listen
    Hoping to be enlightened
    As to their fate
    Seemingly totally

Out of their hands
Confident they will know
Truth when it is presented

People pin all their hopes
    On two statuesque men
    Who would lead them
    Through the dark days
    Watch helplessly
    As they prove to be
    Smaller than their TV images

People sit and wait
    Watch and listen
    To hear the truth
    That shall set them free
    Baffled by the
    Prevarication of those
    Who would lead them

The People wait. . . .

kalaulau valley

THE VALLEY FLOOR rose
    up Taro terraces
    from the ocean
    along the waters flowing
    from the unseen mountaintop
    wettest spot on earth.

Large, flat rocks
    ringed Big Pool,
    nature's drying rack
    after a quick escape
    from the hot humid air
    in the freezing stillness
    of the rapidly flowing stream.

The valley was primeval,
    abundant with trees,
    mango, papaya, guava,
    planted as in a garden,
    seeds spread

by an unseen hand.

As if we are the first
    we walk up the trail
    crisscrossing the stream
    beneath the trees, rising
    until we enter a clearing
    centered in the valley.

Standing there,
    heat from the sun pulling
    moisture from our bare bodies,
    unembarrassed by our nakedness,
    mirrored in each other's eyes,
    we reaffirm our covenant.

happy birthday

MY IMPENDING BIRTHDAY
    a renewal stamp on my birth certificate
    a date I always look forward to.

Each birthday a significant step in life
    carefree childhood to confused teen
    driver's license freedom at sixteen
    legal beer at twenty-one
    dating   courtship   marriage
    parenthood
    middle age crazy
    senior rates at the movies

another date   not yet set
    I don't look forward to
    when "expired" will be stamped
    on my birth certificate

When that fateful day arrives
    I hope the value of my certificate
    will not be measured
    by the years it spans
    but by the life lived.

guilty

WE ARE all murderers
    Cold-blooded killers
    Who care little for others
    Interested only in our own
    Creature comforts
    Ignoring the travails of those
    Close to the ones we murder
    Oh, we didn't pull the trigger ourselves
    Didn't set off the bomb personally
    Yet it was all done with our
    Acquiescence, our complicity
    All so we can have fuel
    For our cars
    Oil for our way of life
    We hear that we are bringing
    Democracy to an oppressed people
    We hear that it will not cost us anything
    We hear everything we want to hear
    We believe everything we hear
    We allow others to act in our name
    We allow others to commit murder
    In our name

Frank Oxarart

We allow ourselves to continue
Our way of life
With no repercussions, no guilt
We don't wash the blood from our hands
We don't even see the blood that flows
From the young men and women
We sent to kill in our name
Who have been killed as well
We don't know the names
Of the murderers or the victims
We don't see that
We are the murderers
We are the victims

poetry

POETRY IS the art
    of seeing with the heart
    rather than the mind.
    A way to reach beyond thought
    clear to the truth.
    Eyes and ears
    can be deceived.
    Taste and touch
    Manipulated.

But the poet's words
    reach deep within,
    past learned norms,
    past universal truths,
    uniting us all
    in one great
    individualistic authenticity
    peculiar to each heartfelt reader.

.

no need

PROGRESS IS WONDERFUL...
    never very good at geography
    now I don't need to be

No need since my world further reduced...
    to a six-inch screen charting my route
    until I get lost then   recalibration

No need for a sense of place or our place in it...
    our world experienced on a 50-inch screen
    Tel Aviv to the Taj Mahal at the press of a button

No need for that trip to the post office...
    email has replaced letter-writing
    though filled with emojis and abbrevs

No need to schlep home from the mall...
    everything we need available online

Frank Oxarart

FedEx UPS and Amazon deliver and return

No need to share a Coke to stay in touch...
    social media keeps our circles of friends
    electronically connected every second

No need for the campus fraternity
    almost all learning can occur online
    degrees electronically conferred

No need to brave rowdy sports crowds...
    our tv   computer   smartphone screens
    provide 50-yard line or courtside seats

No need for coworkers' camaraderie...
    whether at home or abroad
    business can be conducted 24/7

I guess I should be grateful
    for these amazing advances
    I just don't feel the need

my brother bob

ROBERT MICHAEL OXARART
    My younger brother, Bob
    Self-professed Bon Vivant and Raconteur
    I admired his appetite for life
    His all-consuming enthusiasms
    I knew him his entire life
    Yet hearing that he died
    Has left me too close
    To see him clearly
    It's too soon to be able to describe him.

I still start to pick up the phone
    To challenge his political views.
    I stop short of hitting "send."
    About a golf course we should play
    I have no place to send that book.
    He would find interesting, or not.
    I still file items for our ancestral trip
    To the Basque country next year
    A trip I am beginning to realize

Frank Oxarart

We will never make together.

It's too soon.

tracking my day

I **WAKE** as usual
    Full of half-made plans
    Splash water on my face
    Finger comb my hair
    Run the electric toothbrush
    Across my teeth and gums.

Ajax and I set off
    On our morning walk
    Stepping into the moistness
    Of another new day.

Birds flit to and fro
    Hunting for their breakfast
    Calling to each other
    Scolding the squirrels below.

Clouds move from west to east
    Across the lightening expanse

Frank Oxarart

Of another bright new day
Toward the now risen sun.

The waves try to follow
    Are constantly thwarted
    By the sandy shoreline
    Recede, gather force
    Yet again try again
    To follow the clouds.

My dog and I walk along
    Watching the clouds disappear
    Rushing toward new horizons
    Passing the immobile land
    Buffeted by breaking waves.

The sun rises higher in my sky
    Soon passes overhead as
    Breakfast turns to lunchtime
    Dropping low as dinner arrives.

let me tell you

I **USED** to be a man
    I used to be The Man
    led others smothered
    by their Sisyphean task

I climbed higher up the ladder
    saw past the near horizon
    I shared my futuristic vision
    so others too could see

I was The Man
    leader of men and women
    no challenge too great
    always rose to meet the call

I met each morning
    full of energy and purpose
    donned my warrior's suit
    ready to slay the daily dragon

Frank Oxarart

I could tell you of my many deeds
    more bright and shiny in the telling
    than in the doing
    glow more brightly
    each passing day

I led the way
    saw what others could not
    did what others would not
    gave meaning to each day

I tell you
    I was once a man
    I was The Man
    once

let me tell you

I used to be a man . . .

melody de amor

TOGETHER FOR A THIRD of her life,
    She puts the song in my heart.
    Opens so many doors for me,
    Shows me there is a world
    Outside my own, narrow one.
    Teaches me to look at our world,
    Really notice and honor it.
    Stills my mind
    While exciting my soul.
    And in that stillness,
    Explore how to stir my life,
    Shows me how to dare, to be
    Willing to share myself and others.
    Proves the strength and fragility
    Of friendship, far and near.
    Accepts the unconditional love
    Of Caesar, Candy and Ajax,
    Gives back in full measure.
    Nothing is beyond her reach,
    No one is too far to be included.
    She dares to dream,
    Won't sleep until they come true.

Frank Oxarart

    Constantly busy, time for all.

Openness, honesty, loving,
    Hallmarks of her life,
    One that she shares
    Eagerly, with everyone.
    Demands much of herself,
    Demands that you be
    True to yourself,
    Not settle for your sleep,
    But aspire to your dreams.

a tv blessing

BATHED in flickering light
    The wisdom of the ages
    Flows into my body
    My eyes stare raptly
    At the messages
    In the fluttering lines

The past presented
    As a disjointed whole
    Ancient wars morph
    Into present conflicts
    Peoples near and far
    Brought close yet
    Strangely more remote

Totally immersed
    Emotions dulled by the
    Unending repetition of
    Dumbed down history

Frank Oxarart

Current events loop endlessly
Desensitizing me
To the naive inhumanity
Of mankind

what time is it?

LITTLE HAND just past six
    big hand right on the nine
    my alarm clock reads six forty-five

the latest tick counting down
    each moment of my life
    grade school through college
    dates   dances   dalliances
    some serious   some not

my working life
    my married life
    my curious life
    my stale life

Frank Oxarart

On the other hand . . .

if I read the clock face as
    a quarter to seven

I have time to plan ahead . . .
                                  coffee with friends
    weekend in Carmel
            golf at Bandon Dunes
                        roadtrip San Diego to Seattle
      get my kicks on Route 66
  cross Canada by rail
          ski the Sun Valley slopes
                    scale Pike's Peak
        Christmas on Kauai
  sail down the Yangtze River
          cruise the Mediterranean
                  stop in
Spain France Italy Greece

or maybe even dinner and a movie tonight
    six forty-five . . .
    quarter to seven . . .
    It's all in how you look at it.

"pop's gone"

THE VOICE on the phone
    told me my father had died,
    in Mexico, in Ajijic where he lived
    the last dozen years of his life.
    I seldom saw him,
    talked occasionally,
    but got a letter almost every day.
    I could feel the vitality and boredom
    Of his life in his eighties.

In the crematorium,
    lying in the casket,
    was a wrinkled, oaken
    replica of our father,
    less than life-size.
    Lips slightly parted,
    gapped teeth small in his mouth
    eyes closed to his surroundings,
    the skin shrunk from the roots of his hair.

We rummaged through
    the remnants of his life.
    Clothes to the needy,
    books to the library.
    Valuable, important papers
    bagged for the trash man.
    Left the watches on his desk.
    faux Rolexes, Timexes, no names,
    they lay there, undemanding.

tried and true

I'LL TRY USING poetic words this time
    the best words   best order as poets do
    something simple maybe something in rhyme

> *Roses are red*
> *sometimes I'm blue*
> *but strike me dead*
> *if I'm not true*

The Bard compared you to a solitary day
    winter would be cold   could be in the spring
    not the fall   though possibly summer's haze

Elizabeth counted the ways to tabulate
    what's in my heart   just one way won't do
    it's much too long a list to enumerate

Frank Oxarart

Robbie Burns spoke of a Deep Secret rose
    really really red beauty to behold
    fragrant yet too thorny to hold too close

Lord Byron saw you walking slowly at night
    your radiance on view for all to see
    your beauty shining brightly in the moonlight

You lovely bearer of heavenly light
    I can find no Words worthy
    to say you are a specter of delight

With all the words in the dictionary
    I simply fall back on these tried and true
    you're the one for me

I love you.

hometown

I **NAVIGATE** by memory
    rather than street names
    find my way by familiar landmarks
    surer than any GPS.

Past Patsy D'Amore's Restaurant
    now an unfamiliar green and yellow Jose's
    miss the oft-taken turn up the hill
    toward the house we grew up in
    unsettled by a large apartment house
    occupying the once open side yard
    we learned to play football there
    pleased the pool at least still lies
    between the house and brick barbecue.

The wide avenues of my memory
    shrunk to narrow potholed streets
    cars slowly creeping along
    the once imposing office building
    diminished by the chain hotel

next to it near the opulent new mall.

The favorite haunts of my youth
    shrunken now in importance
    ghosts of their once glorious stature
    too crowded   too small   too dingy
    to be the cradle of my youth
    vivid only in my memory
    though that too is beginning to fade.

progress

AS I CHECKED out at Staples yesterday
    I spied an old friend sitting in the corner
    Rand McNally perched on a wire carousel
    a book of highways and byways
    pristine but dusty from disuse
    I once used to plot my travels
    sought potential sightseeing detours
    to enhance the enjoyment of my journey.

Rand McNally replaced by GPS
    territorial outlook narrowed
    to tight telescopic focus
    audio prompts lest I stray.

I check the time on my watch
    could consult my smartphone
    an accurate digital display
    of the exact present moment
    no sense of past or future.

I miss my analog
    unrelenting sweep hands
    showing when it had been
    as well as when it will be
    a circular scan of my day
    time once a leisurely span
    replaced by this instant.

Coffee grounds prepackaged
    my daily beverage in a pod
    I miss choosing my own beans
    grinding them   waiting for them to brew
    the loss of so many simple pleasures
    simply for convenience and progress.

Although I must say
    I find it comforting   monitoring
    your progress with Google Maps
    as you return from Phoenix
    I know precisely how soon
    I will see you dear daughter.

staying in touch

THIS MORNING I got up early again
    fired up the computer in the study
    signed on to both email accounts
    looking for overnight communiques
    opened my iPad and iPhone as well
    checked text messages and voicemail
    nothing new on any device
    not even the old landline telephone.

Last night I gorged on cable news fare
    wanted to know what your take on it was
    contrary to mine of course   it always is
    two sides of government and politics
    that's why we stick to more mundane topics
    Dodgers or Giants   Warriors or Lakers
    courses to play on our next golf odyssey
    where we can get the biggest tastiest ribeye
    scotch or vodka for our twilight decompression.

I settled once again for rereading our old mail

golf trips planned and taken   who won the beers
hiking the French Basque Pyrenees trails
rehashing our parallel broadcast careers.

I reviewed again the pages
    when we planned to chronicle
    the saga of past generations
    in our family tree
    but since you joined them
    I can't bring myself to press delete.

There has been no new mail for several years now
    still I'll check again tomorrow
    just to stay in touch.

wisdom of the aged

THEY SAY wisdom is something to be shared
    So when I had this flash of insight
    Into a problem that affects us all
    Now or in the future
    I felt obligated to share it
    I didn't feel that I could
    In all good conscience
    Keep it to myself just for my benefit
    Some things are too important
    For our sometimes selfish natures

So I am compelled to let as many as possible
    In on my moment of truth
    I hasten to document this bit of intelligence
    So as not to deprive others of its importance
    After all it wouldn't be fair
    That I be the only one to benefit
    From this sudden insight
    It is important to you and to me
    That you pay attention to my revelation

So here goes . . .

I'm just trying to find a way to put it
    Into words that will make it clear
    I know the words would flow freely
    Once I remember exactly what it was
    Just identify the topic or subject matter
    I had this flash of clarity about

I'll just have to think a little harder
    Then I'll be happy to share my
    Newfound intelligence
    I'll just think about it
    A little more

I'll let you know
    Just as soon as I recall
    What I was thinking about

. . . Precisely

meditation at marin

> "All the new thinking is about loss.
> In this it resembles all the old thinking."
> *Meditation at Lagunitas*
> Robert Haas

ROBERT HAAS also wrote that
    reduced to the particular
    the clarity of the general is lost.

I know that now I think mostly about the past.
    In the past I mostly thought about the future.
    What it held for me generally.

However when that future arrived,
    I was living in the particular,
    with all the whys and wherefores
    as to why my particular didn't match
    the promise of my envisioned future.

My thoughts were of opportunities
    lost, which led to an erosion
    of what might have been.
    Thoughts of "if only", "I wish I had",
    "if I knew then, what I know now".
    All the phrases that resonate
    as I contemplate the path
    my particular life has taken.

Yet, given the chance to relive
    all those moments, if it led to
    anything but my life as I know it now,
    I would not make any different choices.

So my new thinking is not about loss,
    but about how my particular life
    is and has been a full life,
    one well worth living generally.

what if

WHEN YOU DIE you get to choose
    A time of your life to cycle through
    Eternally.
    Would you choose that time with
    No responsibilities
    Cared for by your parents
    Dependent for everything.

Would you choose your emerging years
    Grade school, Junior High, High School
    Expanding your circle of friends
    Sinking the winning basket
    Cuddling your first girlfriend
    Driver's license license to explore.

Perhaps you would choose emancipation
    Leaving the nest for the dorm
    Intoxicating independence
    Exploring the world
    Expanding your mind

Frank Oxarart

    Forming forever fraternal friendships.

Maybe you would choose your
    First steps on your career path
    Heady feeling of invincibility
    When you knew intuitively
    All you needed to know
    When all things were possible.

Or would you choose that giddy time
    Your first true love spicing your life
    Creating a homey atmosphere
    To raise your own children
    Balancing home and career
    A purpose to all your efforts.

You might choose the empty nest
    Freedom for you and your wife
    Responsible only to yourselves
    Time to look outward again
    Recharge and expand your horizons
    Spread your wings as they spread theirs.

Would you choose the sudden calm
    As you leave your career
    No more clocks to punch
    Open to newfound leisure
    Time for friends and travel
    Experiences neglected earlier.

What If

When that time comes
    What period of your life
    Would you live
    Again and again
    Through all eternity
    If you could choose?

a bland life

I WAS ALWAYS MORE serene
    on stage behind the curtain
    Puppet master above the scene
    rather than manipulated manikin.

Never liked too spicy a bite
    though a little is often good
    Wore my clothes black and white
    mostly suits never a hood.

My monochromatic pictures
    sepia before their due
    My music solid gold fixtures
    never beat to the new.

Emotions not too high or low
    seldom blue or red
    No hilltop home or valley below

a mid-slope view instead.

But when you chose me
    my life began to soar
    Ahh when you chose me
    the stars were not too far

apologies to walt

HOW WILL you find me
    once I am gone
    ashes to ashes
    I float free on the wind
    sink slowly into the sea
    add nutrients to a tree.

    you will have no need
    to search for me
    I will be with you always
    just as the wind and sea
    and the tree canopy
    comfort and protect you.

www.ingramcontent.com/pod-product-compliance
Lightning Source LLC
Chambersburg PA
CBHW051606010526
44119CB00056B/796